Fact Finders®

DISCOVER THE NIGHT SKY

EXPLORING
METEOR SHOWERS

BY BRIGID GALLAGHER

Consultant:
Ilia Iankov Roussev, PhD

CAPSTONE PRESS
a capstone imprint

Fact Finders Books are published by Capstone Press,
1710 Roe Crest Drive, North Mankato, Minnesota 56003
www.mycapstone.com

Library of Congress Cataloging-in-Publication Data
Library of Congress Cataloging-in-Publication data is available on the Library of Congress website.

978-1-5157-8737-2 (library binding)
978-1-5157-8741-9 (paperback)
978-1-5157-8753-2 (eBook PDF)

Editorial Credits
Adrian Vigliano, editor; Veronica Scott, designer;
Wanda Winch, media researcher; Gene Bentdahl, production specialist

Photo Credits
Alamy Stock Photo: Photo Researchers, Inc., 15, Westend61 GmbH, 24–25; Getty Images: The Denver
Post/Orin Sealy, 22; Newscom: Splash News, 23; Shutterstock: Cylonphoto, cover, Dabarti CGI, 26–27,
Elenarts, 8–9 (background), Everett Historical, 7 (top left), iryna1, 7 (bottom left), Nicku, 7 (right),
Pavel Vakhrushev, starfield background, Pyty, 19 (inset), Rebus_Productions, 17 (inset), shooarts, 5,
SKY2015, 12–13, SkyPics Studio, 6, solarseven, 18–19 (background), turtix, 20–21, Vadim Sadovski, 11
(inset), 16–17 (background); SuperStock: Tony Hallas/Tony Hallas, 10–11 (background); Thinkstock:
iStockphoto/valeriopardi, 8 (inset), iStockphoto/SIYAMA9, 28–29

CONTENTS

CHAPTER 1

WHAT IS A METEOR SHOWER?

Do you ever look up at the night sky? It is very beautiful, especially on a clear night. You can see lots of twinkling lights. Some are stars. Others are planets.

When looking at the sky, do you ever notice how some twinkling lights stay in the same place while others seem to move across the sky? Maybe you've even seen a quick trail of light in the night sky. That is a **meteor**. It is often called a shooting star. Several shooting stars in a short period are called a meteor shower. What causes meteor showers? What can we learn from them? And what do they leave behind? The answers will fascinate you.

Our Solar System

Our solar system circles around the sun. The sun is a star. Earth and the other planets in the solar system revolve around the sun. Other objects in space revolve around the sun too. Some of those objects are **asteroids**, **meteoroids**, and **comets**.

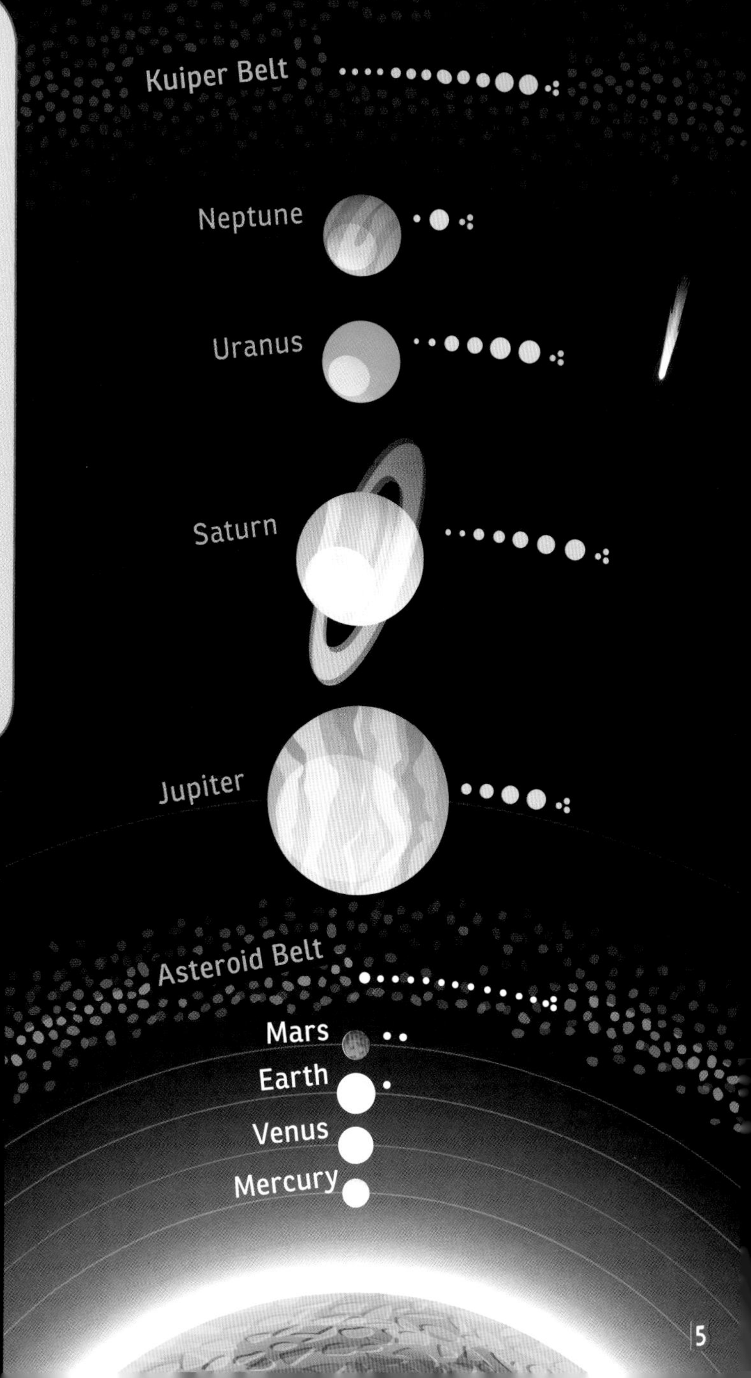

Kuiper Belt

Neptune

Uranus

Saturn

Jupiter

Asteroid Belt

Mars

Earth

Venus

Mercury

meteor—a piece of rock or dust that enters Earth's atmosphere, causing a streak of light in the sky

asteroid—a large space rock that moves around the sun; asteroids are too small to be called planets

meteoroid—rocky or metallic chunk of matter traveling through space

comet—a ball of rock and ice that circles the sun

UNDERSTANDING THE SKY

Since the beginning of time, humans have wanted to know more about outer space. For thousands of years, scientists have worked to understand the solar system. What are those objects in the sky? Why are they there? How were they created? **Astronomy** is the study of these things.

Over time we've been able to answer many questions. We now know that Earth and other planets **orbit** around the sun. The time it takes for Earth to travel around the sun is one year, or 365 days. While Earth is making its way around the sun, it's also spinning on its **axis**. This is an imaginary line that Earth rotates around every 24 hours. It is why we experience daytime and nighttime.

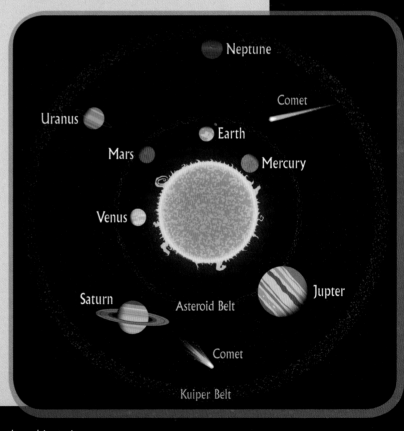

astronomy—the study of stars, planets, and other objects in space
orbit—the path an object follows as it goes around the sun or a planet
axis—a real or imaginary line through the center of an object, around which the object turns

Claudius Ptolemy

Claudius Ptolemy (AD 100–170): Ptolemy lived in Alexandria, Egypt. He wrote a book saying Earth was the center of our solar system and everything revolved around it. Scientists would later prove him wrong.

Nicolaus Copernicus (1473–1543): This Polish scientist published a book in 1543 that questioned if the center of our solar system was not Earth, but the sun.

Nicolaus Copernicus

Galileo Galilei (1564–1642): This Italian genius did a lot of important things during his life. One of his many discoveries happened when he built a telescope. Using it, he collected evidence to prove that the sun is the center of the solar system.

Galileo Galilei

CHAPTER 2

METEORS, ASTEROIDS, AND COMETS

Meteoroids, asteroids, and comets are some of the other objects that orbit the sun. Meteoroids are small particles. Most meteoroids are about the size of a pebble. Sometimes these space rocks hit Earth's **atmosphere** and burn up. This creates a flash of light in the sky. The light usually only lasts for a second. A meteoroid that burns up in Earth's atmosphere is called a meteor.

An object larger than about 33 feet (10 meters) in diameter is called an asteroid. Asteroids are usually made of rock and metal. Comets are similar to asteroids in size, but they are made up of different materials. Comets are usually made of ice, dust, and rock. When a comet orbits close to the sun, its ice turns to vapor and its dust is loosened. These disintegrating materials form a comet's tail.

COMET

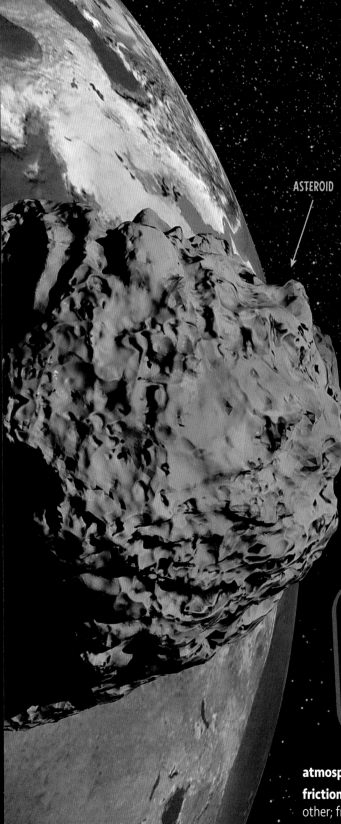

ASTEROID

Earth's atmosphere is a layer of gases (mostly nitrogen and oxygen) that protects and surrounds Earth like a blanket. Meteoroids hit the atmosphere at speeds ranging from 6 to 43 miles (10 to 70 kilometers) per second. The **friction** of a meteor's surface whipping through the atmospheric gases at such high speed causes those gases to ignite. This creates the burning streak of light we see in the night sky.

Did You Know?

Meteoroids are the smallest objects in our solar system. They can be as small as a grain of sand.

atmosphere—the mix of gases that surround a planet
friction—a force produced when two objects rub against each other; friction slows down objects

HIGH IN THE AIR

Sometimes meteors are called shooting stars. The flash of a streaking meteor can look like a star moving across the night sky. But meteors and stars are very different. Stars are made of very hot gases, while meteors are made of rock. Like stars, we can see meteors without help from binoculars or telescopes. It may look like meteors are close to us. But in reality, meteors happen between 50 and 75 miles (80 and 120 km) above Earth's surface.

Even though we can't always see them, meteors are happening all the time. An average of 25 million meteoroids enter Earth's atmosphere every day. It's easier to see meteors on clear nights when we are not surrounded by much city light. Also, our ability to see meteors depends on other factors. The time of year and the tilt of Earth's axis affect how many meteors we can see.

Did You Know?

A fireball is a meteor that is brighter than the average meteor. In fact, fireballs are sometimes brighter than the planets we can see from Earth.

FIREBALL

METEOR SHOWERS

Millions of meteors occur every day. However, there are special times during the year when many can be seen at once in the same part of the sky. During these times, it's as if the meteors are raining down from the sky. These are meteor showers. The showers usually last for a couple of weeks but their peaks, or climaxes, only last a few days.

Comets cause most meteor showers. As comets pass near the sun, materials from their surface disintegrate. This leaves a long trail of meteoroids made from the comet's dust and debris. Some of these meteoroid trails happen to cross Earth's orbit around the sun. When they do, the meteoroids collide with Earth's atmosphere, creating meteor showers. The meteors radiate, or spread, from the point of collision.

Did You Know?

In 1799 American Astronomer Andrew Ellicott Douglass saw the Leonids meteors shower while sailing near the Florida Keys. He described it in his journal, saying that the sky "illuminated with sky rockets, flying in an infinity of directions."

METEOR SHOWER CALENDAR

METEOR SHOWERS OCCUR THROUGHOUT THE YEAR. HERE ARE SOME OF THE MAJOR ONES.

Quadrantids	December/ January	Italian astronomer Antonio Brucalassi first reported this meteor shower in 1825. The peak of action is only a few hours. However, it is considered one of the best annual showers because fireballs are frequent.
Lyrids	April	This is one of the oldest reported meteor showers. It dates all the way back to 687 BC. During this shower the meteors are bright and fast. There are about 10 to 20 meteors per hour.
Eta Aquarids	May	The debris that creates these meteor showers comes from Halley's Comet. It is the most famous comet. During this shower you can see 10 to 30 meteors per hour.
Delta Aquariids	July	This is one of the least intense meteor showers of the year.
Perseids	August	The Perseids is known as the best meteor shower of the year. There are 50 to 100 meteors per hour. The meteors are created from debris from the comet Swift-Tuttle. Fireballs are common, as are meteors with long streaks and color.
Orionids	October	Like the Eta Aquarids, this shower also originates from Halley's Comet. The Orionids is considered one of the most beautiful and fast showers. Around 50 to 70 meteors occur per hour.
Leonids	November	This is a major annual shower. The meteors are frequent and have long, colorful tails. Some are fireballs. Every 33 years, this shower becomes a storm. During a meteor storm, thousands of meteors can be seen per hour.
Geminids	December	Astronomers first reported this shower in the mid-1800s. It is different than other meteor showers. It originates from an asteroid called 3200 Phaethon. About 40 meteors per hour can be viewed.

CHAPTER 3

GUIDE TO WATCHING A METEOR SHOWER

Watching a meteor shower is a lot of fun. However, it's important to know a few things before you do so.

Make a plan with a trusted adult. Find a meteor shower calendar and decide on a meteor shower that you can try to observe. Invite your friends!

Check the weather forecast a few days before your meteor shower. Clouds, rain, and snow will make it difficult for you to see any meteors. A clear sky is ideal when trying to observe space objects. But if the moon is bright, it can be hard to see some meteors.

Get as far away from city lights as possible. If you live in a city or suburb, you will want to go somewhere rural, where there are fewer lights. A dark place to observe the sky is necessary.

Take a nap before you go. You'll be up late! Meteor showers usually reach their peak late in the evening.

Once you have reached your observation location, you'll want to lie back and stare up at the sky. It will take a few minutes for your eyes to adjust to the darkness. Be patient. At first you might only see the brightest objects in the sky. But soon you will see an endless blanket of stars. Finally, you will see the burning streaks of light shooting across the sky.

Did You Know?

Meteor storms occur when you can see around 1,000 meteors per hour, sometimes even more! The most famous meteor storm happened on November 12 and 13, 1833. It is known as the great Leonid Meteor Storm. During the nine-hour storm, about 240,000 meteors were seen. That's over 26,000 meteors per hour! This storm was intense. After it, many scientists focused more attention on studying meteors.

CHAPTER 4

STONES FROM THE SKY

Sometimes meteors do not completely burn up when they pass through Earth's atmosphere. Instead, the debris falls from the sky to Earth. When this debris lands on the ground, it is known as **meteorites**. Most meteorites discovered on Earth are pebble-sized to fist-sized. But some have been as large as buildings!

Where are these meteorites? All over Earth! Many meteorites land in water and are never recovered. People have found meteorites in very cold regions, such as Antarctica and Greenland. Meteorites also land in very hot, dry regions, such as deserts. More than 50,000 meteorites have been discovered and studied all over the world.

Types of Meteorites

There are three main types of meteorites: stony, iron, and stony-iron. Stony meteorites are the most common. About 94 percent of all meteorites found on Earth are stony. Iron meteorites are much less common but are easier to recognize. They don't look like regular rocks. Stony-iron meteorites are made of stone and metal. They are extremely rare. Almost all meteorites — 99.8 percent — come from asteroids. The other 0.2 percent of meteorites comes from Mars and the moon.

Iron Meteorite

Did You Know?

Meteorites range in age from 200 million years old to 4.5 billion years old! They help provide evidence to **astronomers** of when and how the solar system was formed.

meteorite—a piece of meteor that falls all the way to the ground
astronomer—a scientist who studies stars, planets, and other objects in space

FAMOUS METEORITES

Some meteorites have become famous among astronomers. These are just a few of the world's most important meteorites.

Sylacauga Meteorite (Hodges Meteorite)

On November 30, 1954, near Sylacauga, Alabama, a meteorite hit a human. Such an event is extremely rare. Ann Hodges was in her home napping. Suddenly an 8.5-pound (3.9-kg) stony meteorite crashed through her roof. It hit her hip, leaving a big bruise. Although the meteorite was worth a lot of money, Ann kept it for herself. She used it as a doorstop!

Willamette Meteorite

Scientists believe that the Willamette Meteorite landed at least 13,000 years ago. Researchers believe it struck Earth somewhere in Montana or Canada and eventually was moved to Oregon by glaciers. It is the biggest meteorite found in North America. It is made of mostly iron and a little nickel. It can now be seen at the American Museum of Natural History in New York City. American Indians from the Willamette Valley refer to it as "Tomonowos," or "the visitor from the sky."

Allan Hills 84001 (ALH 84001)

On December 27, 1984, a group of American scientists discovered this meteorite in Allan Hills, Antarctica. They were on a mission specifically to find meteorites. They succeeded in more ways than one. The meteorite was special. Scientists now say there is evidence that Allan Hills 84001 was once a part of the planet Mars. They believe that another meteorite hit the surface of Mars and blasted Allan Hills 84001 into orbit around the sun. About 13,000 years ago its orbit brought it close to Earth and it crashed onto Earth's surface.

Hoba Meteorite

The Hoba is an iron meteorite found in 1920 in South West Africa (now Namibia). It is the largest meteorite ever discovered. It weighs an estimated 60 tons (54,431 kilograms)! Scientists believe that the Hoba fell to Earth 80,000 years ago. It is now a national Namibian monument site. Many people visit it each year.

Hoba Meteorite

CRATERS

Sometimes a meteorite creates a bowl-shaped hole when it hits Earth. This hole is called an impact **crater**. The hole can be deep, or it can be wide and ridged. Impact craters do not happen very often on Earth. Even so, researchers have confirmed about 190 impact craters on our planet.

One of the most famous impact craters is near Winslow, Arizona. It is known as the Meteor Crater or Barringer Crater. Geologist Daniel Barringer spent many years proving that a meteorite caused the crater. The crater is very large. It's 560 feet (171 m) deep and almost a mile wide. It was formed around 50,000 years ago. The Barringer family now owns the crater, but is open to the public for viewing.

Another famous crater is estimated to be around 65 million years old! The Chicxulub is 180 miles (290 km) wide. The meteorite that formed it landed in Mexico on the Yucatan Peninsula. Most scientists believe that it contributed to extinction, or loss, of various animals on Earth, including the dinosaurs.

crater—bowl-shaped landform created by a meteorite crashing into a planet

CHAPTER 5

LEARNING FROM METEORITES

Meteorites teach us many things about our planet and solar system. But they haven't always been given the attention they deserve. In fact, it wasn't until the 1930s that scientists began to study meteorites more closely. We have Harvey H. Nininger to thank for that.

Harvey H. Nininger

Harvey Nininger taught biology at McPherson College for ten years. In 1923 he saw a fireball in the sky. It was a life-changing event. After this sight he decided to devote his time to discovering meteorites. He believed that studying meteorites could help us to better understand our solar system and **universe**. He was right.

Nininger's studies were so interesting that more scientists began to take notice. Nininger taught people that meteorites were much more common on Earth than previously believed. By the 1940s, he was responsible for half of all the meteorite discoveries in the world.

The British Museum owns half of Nininger's meteorite collection. He sold it to them in 1958. The other half of his collection is at the Arizona State University Center for Meteorite Studies. Many of the space rocks are displayed in their museum for people to view.

universe—everything that exists, including Earth, the planets, the stars, and all of space

LOOKING FOR METEORITES

To see meteors and meteor showers we look up at the sky. To see meteorites we must look down at the ground. There are many different types of stones and rocks on the ground. When you're looking for a meteorite, it's important to know a few things first.

1. Meteorites fall everywhere on Earth, but there are places where they're easier to spot. These include very dry, hot areas such as deserts and very cold, icy locations.

2. Bring a magnet! Most meteorites are made of iron and nickel and have magnetic pull.

3. Know what to look for. Study photos of meteorites. Many look burnt on the outside and are dark brown or black. Also, they are usually very solid, not crumbly like some stones.

You can view meteorites all over the world. Some people purchase meteorites for their private collections. Special meteorites are usually housed in natural history museums. The largest collections of meteorites are at the Smithsonian Institution in Washington, D.C. and the National Institute of Polar Research in Tokyo, Japan. If you don't live close to one of these cities, you can probably see a meteorite at your local natural history museum.

METEOR STUDIES TODAY

Some organizations continue to track meteors. These include the American Meteor Society, The Meteoritical Society, and the European Fireball Network. These groups track and record all reported night sky movement. Lists of meteors, fireballs, comets, and asteroids are on their websites. Government organizations such as NASA have technology that detects meteors in different regions.

NASA has successfully explored areas to find rare meteorites. On a trip in Antarctica in the early 1980s, NASA scientists found meteorites from the moon — called lunar meteorites. Lunar meteorites were blasted away from the moon's surface by the impact of an asteroid or meteoroid. Some of them entered orbit around Earth, and eventually made their way through the atmosphere and crashed to the surface.

Did You Know?

In 1794 German physicist Ernst Chladni published the first book on meteorites. In it he theorized that meteorites were rocks from space. He was not taken seriously until about 10 years later. At that point, French scientist Jean-Baptiste Biot and British chemist Edward Howard had proven Chladni's theory. Meteorites were, in fact, from outer space.

UNDERSTANDING OUR UNIVERSE

Studying meteoroids, meteors, and meteorites helps us to understand more about the history of the planetary system. Thanks to meteorites, we know that our solar system is 4.6 billion years old. They've also allowed us to discover the composition of planets, moons, asteroids, and more. These space rocks have been key in uncovering information about our world. All sorts of people — from average citizens to scientists — can make meteorite discoveries. Each new discovery improves our knowledge and understanding of the universe.

Next time you see a meteor in the night sky or watch a meteor shower, think about all that we know thanks to those beautiful, brief flashes of light.

Did You Know?

The Arizona State University Center for Meteorite Studies has the largest collection of meteorites of any other university in the world.

GLOSSARY

asteroid (AS-tuh-royd)—a large space rock that moves around the sun; asteroids are too small to be called planets.

astronomy (uh-STRAH-nuh-mee)—the study of stars, planets, and other objects in space

atmosphere (AT-muhss-fihr)—the mix of gases that surrounds a planet

axis (AK-siss)—a real or imaginary line through the center of an object, around which the object turns

comet (KOM-uht)—a ball of rock and ice that circles the sun

crater (KRAY-tuhr)—bowl-shaped landform created by a meteorite crashing into a planet

friction (FRIK-shuhn)—a force produced when two objects rub against each other; friction slows down two objects and heats them up.

meteor (MEE-tee-ur)—a piece of rock or dust that enters Earth's atmosphere, causing a streak of light in the sky

meteorite (MEE-tee-ur-ite)—a piece of meteor that falls all the way to the ground

meteoroid (MEE-tee-ur-oyd)—rocky or metallic chunk of matter traveling through space

orbit (OR-bit)—the path an object follows as it goes around the sun or a planet

universe (YOO-nuh-verss)—everything that exists, including Earth, the planets, the stars, and all of space

READ MORE

Atkinson, Stuart. *Comets, Asteroids, and Meteors.* Astronaut Travel Guides. Chicago: Raintree, 2013.

Lawrence, Ellen. *Comets, Meteors, and Asteroids: Voyagers of the Solar System.* Zoom into Space. New York: Ruby Tuesday Books Ltd., 2013.

Stewart, Melissa. *Meteors.* National Geographic Kids. Washington, D.C.: National Geographic, 2015.

INTERNET SITES

Use FactHound to find Internet sites related to this book.

Visit *www.facthound.com*

Just type in 9781515787372 and go.

Check out projects, games and lots more at
www.capstonekids.com

CRITICAL THINKING QUESTIONS

1. How have meteorites helped scientists determine the age of our solar system?

2. What are the differences between meteoroids, meteors, and meteorites?

3. When is the next meteor shower? Use the Internet to research nearby places that offer a good view of the night sky. Make a plan to see the shower for yourself!

INDEX